Pe

PEARSON

Glenview, Illinois • Boston, Massachusetts • Chandler, Arizona
Upper Saddle River, New Jersey

Here are two pet helpers.
They help pets.
Do you know what they do?

This man is a dog trainer.
He works in a puppy school.
He teaches dogs to be good.

Take your dog to a puppy school.
A trainer can teach your dog.
Your dog can be good, too.

This dog is good.
The trainer teaches the dog.
He teaches the dog to sit.

This woman is a vet.
A vet is a doctor for animals.
Vets help all kinds of animals.

The vet helps sick pets.
She helps pets that are hurt.
Pets need to be healthy.

Puppy trainers and vets like pets.
That is why they are pet helpers.
How can you help a pet?